COUNTRY OF ARRIVAL

PREVIOUS BOOKS BY HUBERT MOORE

Down by a Bicycle, Hippopotamus Press, 1979
Namesakes, Enitharmon Press, 1988
Rolling Stock, Enitharmon Press, 1991
Left-Handers, Enitharmon Press, 1995
Touching Down in Utopia, Shoestring Press, 2002
The Hearing Room, Shoestring Press, 2006
Whistling Back, Shoestring Press, 2012
The Bright Gaze of the Disoriented, Shoestring Press, 2014
The Tree Line, Shoestring Press, 2017
The Feeding Station, Shoestring Press, 2019
Owl Songs, Shoestring Press, 2021

COUNTRY OF ARRIVAL

HUBERT MOORE

All rights reserved. No part of this work covered by the copyright herein may be reproduced or used in any means – graphic, electronic, or mechanical, including copying, recording, taping, or information storage and retrieval systems – without written permission of the publisher.

Printed by imprintdigital
Upton Pyne, Exeter
www.digital.imprint.co.uk

Typesetting and cover design by The Book Typesetters
us@thebooktypesetters.com
07422 598 168
www.thebooktypesetters.com

Published by Shoestring Press
19 Devonshire Avenue, Beeston, Nottingham, NG9 1BS
(0115) 925 1827
www.shoestringpress.co.uk

First published 2022
© Copyright: Hubert Moore
© Cover painting: Nasrin Parvaz
© Photograph of painting: Darrie Payne

The moral right of the author has been asserted.

ISBN 978-1-915553-05-8

ACKNOWLEDGEMENTS

Several of these poems have been published before. Acknowledgements are due to the editors of 'Poetry and Settled Status for all' (Civil Leicester), 'The North', 'The Salzburg Review', 'Scintilla'.

Many thanks to Nasrin Parvaz for her painting on the front cover and to Darrie Payne for his photograph of the painting. I have been lucky to have had such excellent designers as The Book Typesetters working on the collection.

Most of all I want to say how much I owe to John Lucas of Shoestring Press who, eight times now, has given me peace of mind about publication and thus the space and confidence to write to my heart's content.

CONTENTS

Section One
'SPLASH OFF BACKWARDS'

Chimney piece	3
Launching	4
Fireplace	5
From the side	6
To swim	7
At the pond's edge	8
Running out	9

Section Two
'INCOMERS'

Greeting	13
Crossing blind	14
Crawling under	15
Hollyhock	16
Mixing in	17
Sea-pictures	18
The Threatfish	19
A silent insistence	20
Weather Front	21
Consultation Document	22
Undersides	23
Volcanoes	24
Running already	25
Bales appear	26
Snakes and ladders	27
In the mist	28

Section Three
'PEOPLE GET RARER'

In a field between woods	31
Walking out	32
The Charge of the Care Brigade	33
All the difference	34
Single file	35
Learning back	36
The music of all clear	37

Section Four
'ALMOST SPENT VOLCANO'

Extract	41
Removals	42
Ascension	43
The toppling	44
Leave to remain	45
The road taken	46
Defending the castle	47
In the desert	48
Slippers	49
Gifts from Australia	50
Scars of not	51

Section Five
'FIELD OF VISION'

The heart and the hearing	55
Unmuted	56
Law	57
Cold baths	58
Reaching, being reached	59
The only place	60
Field of vision	61
Pure post	62
Back-licking	63
As goldfinches	64
Work in progress	65
Leg before	66
The log-man	67

Section One

'Splash off backwards'

CHIMNEY PIECE

Quite often in the summer
when the stove's unlit
something falls struggling upward
down the chimney where it
can't go anywhere. Waits there
throbbing. All it needs is words.

LAUNCHING

You hear the scuffle
of what might be wings
then not just scuffling
but a body flinging
at the glass door of a stove.

Yesterday when I opened
a young blackbird knew
exactly where the window
of the sitting-room was
and flew straight out un-

altered. Some aren't like this,
need so much work on them,
blankets blocking exits
which go nowhere, re-
starting, coaxing to

the edge of the outside
world where the sky begins
which isn't window, isn't
glass but air-space open
like an open book.

FIREPLACE

The fireplaces they used to
build in bedroom walls
weren't follies though

they must have been a danger
to the bedding. Ours is three feet
from where I sleep.

Some days the decorative
ironwork round its open
mouth is what I first stare

out at. Still busy
in the busy-ness of sleep,
the knowing, the forgetting,

I wake to how our fire
must have been so adept
in its drawing up

of flame, of smoke
that now it draws up half-
made fragments which dis-

integrate if morning
light or I reach out
and try to touch them.

FROM THE SIDE

At last I've found the perfect
toothpaste tube, damaged
maybe in our bathroom,

maybe in the factory
where they must be searching
for perfection all the time.

There's a half-inch skin-split
just below the nozzle.
You don't untwist, you squeeze.

No one really wants
to be dictated to, no one
wants toothpaste coming

at them in their face. Better
to let it leak out sideways,
hint at, not quite say.

TO SWIM

Sometimes you can't let go
of the ladder and when you do

you splash off backward
for a stroke or two then

struggle back. You don't
go anywhere that's not

provisional, anywhere
you can't get back from

to a blank white page.
To set off across the lake

and let the breathing
of your whispered words

transport you, take you stroke
by stroke, each line of you

easing through nothingness
and into each next line,

that would be buoyancy,
that would be to swim.

AT THE POND'S EDGE

Maybe you never change,
you don't move on
from when you first

do watering. You used
to kneel beside the pond
and press

your can against its surface
till it let you in.
You didn't have to

press too hard, it seemed
to want to make a space
for you and then come

swarming into it. That
kneeling by the pond, that going
deeper stays with me

as does the gritty blackish
pondwater I poured out
on the plants. I would have

knelt and filled my pen with it
and written this poem
long before I wrote it

if I'd had no sense.

RUNNING OUT

I'm running out, my pen
can hardly spare the ink
to write about a ragged
line of geese strung out
across the sky and down
behind a clump of trees
beyond me. One by one
I'm running out of them.
They must be streaming off
into my nib and coming
through it to the gleaming
calm of being written
down on paper.

Section Two

'Incomers'

GREETING

(i)

My grandfather loved greeting,
standing outside his house
beside the road his long
black overcoat hanging
heavy. When we arrived
he buried our soft faces
in the rough of it. We
were the young, the incomers.
We loved even the bristles,
even the coarse material
of the overcoat my grandfather
would wear when greeting.

(ii)

Research has shown
the distance the father
of the prodigal son
runs in his eagerness
to greet his son
when he is still far off
is the same 25 miles
as between Dover
and where the displaced
wait in the woods
near the coast of France.
Same joys, same journey.

CROSSING BLIND

The stranded ones not even
written yet and not
yet smuggled through

are crossing blind.
They have a still sea-mist
to blind them, to let them

work their way across
unseen. It's no good
if they set their sights

on endings, on white cliffs.
They've no sights to set,
they've nothing but a sea

of little chasms behind them
opened like mouths, like wounds
closed over now,

and underneath their boat
a sea of stillness
to be paddled through.

CRAWLING UNDER

Two wasps came
searching for family,

not bent double in someone's
lorry, not longing

for the crunch of pebbles
under a boat

but squeezing in through
hardly opened windows,

finding the nest
destroyed, the family gone.

What wasps do to make
up a life to crawl into,

what these two did
was crawl round walls

of a room beneath
where the nest used to be,

crawl where the walls
meet the ceiling, crawl

under and only fly
if they have to.

HOLLYHOCK

A hollyhock arrived
from nowhere, sowed itself
and grew two stems of pale

pink flowers. No way
of telling where
it started from or what

it went through to
grow here but when
in its final flowering

a hurricane blew up
you knew by how
it bowed and swayed

and went along with any-
thing the storm
could do to beat it down

that some pale vein
in hollyhocks
had learnt about being beaten

and surviving
even before it drifted
in and settled here.

MIXING IN

Beneath the stained old sheet
of canvas which keeps our compost
not too hot in summer, not too cold
in winter, two blindworms
have appeared from nowhere
and have made a home. Somehow
when you pull the canvas back
you expect the courtesy
of alarm, a slither off
and down some mushy slipway.
We'd think more kindly of them
cowering out of sight.
Good for blindworms how
they lie back in our mix
of peelings, cuttings, coffee-grounds
and (if they had eyes) stare
into us and through us.

SEA-PICTURES
for Nasrin

We have your seas
in almost every room.
Green sea, blue sea, almost
fiery sea and each sea
as your paint imagines it
has an overloaded boat
too deep in it and people
with pins for heads huddled
tiny in all that swell.

These seas you paint, are they
the sea your parents
used to take you children to
from Tehran in summer
holidays? Or are they all
the multi-mooded sea
we stare at from a seaside
bench in Whitstable?

THE THREATFISH

Late night party-goers
report from Dover
an unusual purring past
of something in the Channel.
They hadn't seen it. No
overloaded boats had come
to join the party. The purring

went off west and sure enough
early morning swimmers
had to share the beach at Folkestone
with a huge white fish. It had
a toothy grinning face, a newly
painted weather-boarded body,
windows for eyes and a hatch

for getting in or out. From here
emerged a rampant Threat Commander
threatening with other rampant
threateners stooping out behind.
The swimmers finished swimming
got out, made room, went home
for breakfast duly threatened.

A SILENT INSISTENCE

Sometimes you hear
beyond your own heart breaking
the silences
between the punch and punch
of breaking waves.

Easy to miss
in all the undermining
backwash washing over
what silence
as the fleeing people

haul themselves from overloaded
dinghies on your shore
must be mouthing at you.
No illegality.
No threat.

WEATHER FRONT

It had to come, couldn't keep
chasing its tail out there
being swirled, swirling.

You could follow the sweep
of the weatherman's hand
round and into our country.

Turn our backs if we must,
turn our faces towards it.
Nothing can stop the dotted

line of its coming,
of wanderers, searchers, seekers,
people soon to be us

as we switch on the news,
flick flat stones across water,
hang washing out in the wind.

CONSULTATION DOCUMENT

Gangs of rodents
are ripping down our fences,
burrowing under, letting
lambs come in. We've always
loved our lambs but this time
for safety's sake and to ensure
the gangs of criminals
leave our shores for ever
the government has decided
to eliminate all lambs.
Full compensation will be paid
to butchers, owners of abattoirs,
sheep-farmers. The government
values your opinion. Please
tick the appropriate box.
How effective do you think
the decision to eliminate
lambs will be (a) effective
(b) very effective (c) very very
effective?

UNDERSIDES

Wind came, only a breezy
ripple but enough
to be a problem for
clandestine Channel threats,
for people in small boats
crossing from France to England
in their search for safety.

Twelve miles back from the beaches
it's breezy enough
to flip the leaves up
of a row of poplars.
What you see is under-
sides turned inside out,
truth white in the wind.

VOLCANOES

Found several small volcanoes
in the garden. One of them
was live, no mole but the soil

was quaking, arching up,
almost falling open.
If rocks and dust and ashes

have nowhere else to go
but up then what can we
not hope for, earth-

encrusted fingers then
the crown of someone's head
erupting, arching up

from having fled, from
tunnelling blindly through
to anywhere, to here?

RUNNING ALREADY

Running already, trusting,
facing forward, when the

baton comes your hand
held out behind you, fingers

curled like pliers before
snapping shut on what's

been thrust in them. No
questions asked, you know

betrayal's bullet shape.
You have to go with it, with

help that doesn't help
or maybe to be people-

smuggled through in what
a smuggled person said

was kindness. People helping
other people, very good.

BALES APPEAR

Dropped at random
in a foreign field
their pale round faces
blank. So whirled about
they seem, maybe their pasts
can't settle in their heads
or else at last they've

come and find their word
for this stares back
at them and knows it's
not enough for all
the months, the years
of fleeing, edging forward,
stumbling here today.

SNAKES AND LADDERS

You thought you'd learned to play
the games dictators play.

Hide and Seek of course though
Hide and Not Be Found is where

you kept your special skill.
One morning you weren't anywhere.

When the men came seeking
you'd already carried off

your freedom in a little
boat. UK you came to but

you'd hardly got here when quite
courteously they asked you to play

Snakes and Ladders with them. It
was Snakes for you. You travelled

in a boat so dangerous, they said,
you have to leave at once.

You should have come by ladder,
arriving at Heathrow.

IN THE MIST

Out in the mist toward Essex
fifty or so on a windfarm.

Long lean blades revolving
over the grey of the sea. No

leaking dinghies, no border-
boats swooping to stop them.

The earthly, the un-
miraculous, flounders here,

can't share the same sea
as these mildly proceeding

walkers on water. Dear
refugees in the mist, walk

on water across to us,
save us, save us from us.

Section Three

'People get rarer'

IN A FIELD BETWEEN WOODS

After Edward Thomas' poem,' As the team's head-brass', written 105 years before this one.

Near the top of the hill
there's the diamond shape of a field
between two woods.

You can't see all of it
not from down in the valley in 2020
where we've got to now.

Edward Thomas' lovers have disappeared
not quite *into the woods*
but at the far end of the field

in the trees' privacy.
As precarious here as in 1915
the love they make, the promises.

In the field between woods
in the gap between hoping and sickness
they have nothing but now to love with.

WALKING OUT

How rare and beautiful the walkers are
when distancing along the path across the field.
Singles, couples most of them

going slowly, dawdling even. They seem
to want the footpath to go on
and on. It's too far off for us

to see the beauty in their faces,
only the way they walk like trees
would walk erect adoring light.

Also how they unlock their branches
into open sky not so much to point
as to come out clear-cut.

Every day the death-toll rises
people get rarer and more beautiful.

THE CHARGE OF THE CARE BRIGADE

Tennyson's poem of 1854 gives 600 as the number of Light Brigade soldiers sent to an almost certain death. The number of Care Home deaths in UK in 2020 is more like 20,000.

These were the chosen,
the dear, the devoted,
grandparent, citizen
coolly promoted.
Their's not to make reply,
their's not to reason why,
their's but to yield and die.
Someone had blundered,
no one had shielded
these more than six hundred.

Frailest of vanguards
leading us onwards.
Tories to left of them,
Tories to right of them,
Tories in front of them
vaunting with war-words.
All the world wondered
how these so vulnerable
entered the mouth of hell,
these more than six hundred.

ALL THE DIFFERENCE

A man we know
knows all the difference
difference can make. Iraqi Kurd
trained as a paramedic in Iraq,
refugee to Britain, carer,
Care Home Manager now.

Fifteen years ago was taken
handcuffed from a cell in Colnbrook
to be deported. A friend, a lawyer
and a technicality slipped in
across the border and with only
minutes till the plane took off

saved him. He knew all
the difference then and knew
it too when on the 1st of March
this year, not on the 23rd,
he chose with full approval
from the relatives his Care Home's

own lockdown. The difference
that the difference made is like
taut-stretched razor-wire
between this and that. Carers
and cared for, not one became
infected, not one died.

SINGLE FILE

There was a track
flattened with shoeprints
pointing where to go.

We followed blind
like water falling forward
onto water.

Six weeks, six months
so long as we could walk
together if not arm-

in-arm then ear-
to-ear. We could whittle
lives we would have lived

down to the peeled white
point of being. We should
have realized there'd be

no one winding down
the path across the mountains,
no returners

who at least could say
how far, how long and when
the high ground came

we would be one and one
and each a separated
breathing self.

LEARNING BACK

You said that once a week
you let yourself come out
of isolation and you went
masked by Underground
to art class. You couldn't
stay at home, you had
things to learn you said.

Down in the underground of words
you meant another thing.
Every week you needed
to learn back the look
in people's eyes unmasked,
staring at nowhere,
frightened, calm.

THE MUSIC OF ALL CLEAR

Nothing we could do.
Every childhood night
for years it seems
the air-raid sirens howled
and every night we heard
the growl of bombers
drilling through the dark
to Coventry. We lay
directly underneath them
hardly even whispering,
waiting in silence
for the music of all clear.

All clear is never all
and never clear. Variants
wait to hear its music
and sirens still howl past us
to the hospital.

Section Four

'Almost spent volcano'

EXTRACT

Copying someone's words
about the scandal
of detention I can't
expect my arty
long-nibbed needle-pen
to extract a milli-
gram of the pain
detention causes.

Only that the paper
I'm writing on
absorbs my ink
so everyone who stoops
to read from it
inhales its understanding,
is infected by it,
breathes its breath.

REMOVALS

Nothing to be ashamed of,
crates of cutlery and books,
mattresses, whole beds, tables,
rigid air-extracted clothes-bags,
pots and pots of plants. Far
from it the van they use
announces it to all the other
traffic unashamed and no one
says they don't believe it,
no one asks what's being
removed. Can't be people,
crates of men, bags which might
have women in them, pots
and pots of children being
taken off in unmarked vans
and then flown back to where
they fled from, sometimes back
to where they've never been.

ASCENSION

Can't believe we've sunk so low,
risen to such extremities
of caring for ourselves
and no one else, we even
think of using a left-over
of empire, a small volcanic
island in the Atlantic
to build a cage for people
who come to us for help
in little boats. Can't believe
we'd fly them off 4000 miles
to make them breathe the smoke
of inhumanity the almost
spent volcano of us
sends rising filthily.

THE TOPPLING

Never thought we'd live to see
it actually topple over.
Upturned the statue fell
across the square, its
staring face, its uprightness
in pieces, skidding, strewn
amongst us. On a slab worked
loose, 'In recognition,' it says,
'of the achievement' (maybe
they'll lock the plaque away
until we need to say such things
again) 'of establishing
in the heart of Africa
detention camps for illegal
immigrants to Britain.'

LEAVE TO REMAIN

Leave to remain is everything
and nothing. It's what you long for
but its small print doesn't
mention what you leave behind
when you remain.

Home smells, the lingering
of sounds. Some have to tell
themselves they'll never pass
their new-born child across
to grandparents to hold.

Every refugee has the story
of a refugee behind them.
How to leave your story,
leave the name of refugee
behind and be, happen

to be a person who drives taxis,
a person watching swans
fly overhead, a person
whose first thought on waking
is of a sleeping child.

THE ROAD TAKEN
for Nasrin

Last time we spoke you said Frost's
'The Road Not Taken', the road
along which you would have walked
free of prison, exile, life-long pain
was currently your favourite poem.
Both of you took the other road,
'the one less travelled by'. I don't know
why, I think Frost must have
found himself taking the other
and went on taking it. You,
I'm hardly the one to pronounce,
found yourself too. Found the ex-
quisite self we've come to admire
though maybe that self is where
all your roads would have led.

DEFENDING THE CASTLE

Someone had left a medi-
eval sandcastle half-
fortified half-finished
on the beach at Margate.
Its moat still needed bucket-
fuls to fill it, its sand-walls
needed plastering with sand.
Between their glances at how
fast the rising tide would sweep
across the beach towards them
three who had come to UK
from Iraq, Darfur, Afghanistan
could hardly stand or speak
for helpless laughter, couldn't
stop their walls collapsing,
their castle being washed away.
Indifference, welcome back.
They'd known genocide, these three,
had fought it and had fled.

IN THE DESERT

Even at night your camels
knew the way across the desert
to the market where you sold
your latest load of mangoes.
We almost knew it too,
no lights, no road, no signposts,
only moon and stars and camel-sense
and like an undipped headlamp
your delighted expertise.

In UK after prison
then detention, you found a place
in destitution, standing
only in a telephone box
in Shepherd's Bush. Even this
was nothing to the eerie
desert in North London where
they found a room for you
which no one else would occupy.

SLIPPERS

One Christmas you and I
were each presented with a pair
of bedroom slippers, size 12
for your feet, broad and baked
in tingling hot Sahara sand,
and for mine. Ten years
before these slippers I had tried
your broadness on, entered
your huge capacity for brave-
facing anything. I had
to tell you your whole family
had been killed. Small-voiced,
a no one in the cave of you,
I said it. I can't ask you
if you took your slippers
back with you. I want to know,
Did you shuffle off to bed
that evening the night before
they shot you in Darfur?

GIFTS FROM AUSTRALIA

You loved Australia,
you brought back brightly painted
boomerangs in plenty
for your English friends.

I still don't understand
why when you throw them
boomerangs skim off and round
and back to you, why

when you're back in London
and we hear you're using
your Uber-driving earnings
to rebuild damaged

wells in villages in Darfur
we can't help welling too
with, is it pride, this
brightly painted gift

you left us with or
is it your great-heartedness,
lonely, skimming back
to find us now you're gone?

SCARS OF NOT
for Sharif Barko (1962–2021)

We weren't there
when they shot you dead
three thousand miles away.
Safe in our beds at home
we still weren't out of range.

The last live picture
has you sitting totally
unsafe at ease among
your friends. Your smile straight
at the camera lures us

across to feel your hug
of reassurance round us.
We come to your memorial
sitting at a screen
where no one sees

the scars, the bullet-wounds
of loving you, of having
no burn-marks on our backs,
of not being tortured,
not shot dead ourselves.

Section Five

'Field of vision'

THE HEART AND THE HEARING
for Danyah

The doctors at the hospital
closed the hole in your heart
and opened up your hearing.

Now you can start again.
When you get home there'll be
soft nonsense - can you hear it? -

coming from your parents.
There'll be the little trills
of sound your brothers make.

They're words, the sort of music
you'll be playing soon. Don't
think of meanings. The heart

will understand. Your ears
throbbing with endearments,
your heart hearing.

UNMUTED

When we got to school
they ticked our names off,
muted us although
we hardly needed it,
the other frightened boys
and I in 1945, set us
a hymn to sing, some
education to be going
on with and we floated
silently along with it
where we were pointed.

Unmuting someone
can't be done to order,
switching on or off. All
we did was face the other
way. We hardly made
a splash for twenty
years and then in rougher
narrower water
a jam of logs came
bursting down my river
jostling to be said.

LAW

Our Latin teacher only
had initials, didn't have
a first name or a surname,
only LAW. He'd written
books on Latin grammar
which we learnt for homework.
Learn by heart, he'd tell us,
all the Latin prepositions
and which case they take.
He was our preposition.
We came after him, his
Cases, his Accusatives,
his Ablatives. Never
suspected there'd be
other laws of grammar
waiting to be followed
if ever what we needed
was to write our minds.

COLD BATHS
at a Methodist boys' boarding school 1950

At 6 am John Wesley used to tip-
toe through our dormitory
and run our baths for us.

Cold baths, I can hear the steady
deepening of the water's voice
as the baths filled.

We didn't mind the cold,
kept our gasps to ourselves.
Quite soon we'd toughen up

and not know what gasps were.
We didn't have to feel
our feelings, we needn't

tremble, blush or weep.
We could keep a safe white
silence going for weeks.

REACHING, BEING REACHED
for Susie

Took my latest book
down the road to where
our favourite neighbour lives.
Knocked, no answer, knocked. Slid
my poems through her letter-

box and heard them landing
on the other side. Came home.
The hole I hadn't yet got
round to digging in the garden
looked up at me. Such silence

going on between things. As when
that evening I didn't hear
our neighbour knocking, not
being invited in. Later
I opened our front door

to five tall sticks of rhubarb
stiff with reaching up for light.
No words needed. All of us -
we plants, we human beings -
love reaching, love being reached.

THE ONLY PLACE

The only place of safety
is the poem itself. You flee
from speechlessness, white spaces,
and if you're lucky the city
of sanctuary takes you in.

If you're lucky there's no leak
in the boat you've hired,
no avalanche blocking the path
you take across the mountains,
no border-guard awake

and no righteous booted men
climbing your precipice of stairs
at 5 a.m., kicking your door in,
twisting your words until
they howl their innocence.

Once inside your room, inside
your table-lamp's kind glow,
you learn to mean the words
your poem speaks for you, your
lines go sauntering out

across the chasms of white
silence that you fled from.
Asylum is an ink
you dip your pen into
and write your leave to remain.

FIELD OF VISION

The field of vision
that gloved and padded up
you walk out on to
at the ophthalmologist's
operates through sparks of light
appearing and you acknowledging
every spark you see.

Gully, mid-off, mid-on
you can't help seeing them.
It's deep square leg, deep extra cover, deep third man
that interest the ophthalmologist.

Maybe I did miss them. Maybe my field
of vision's getting narrower
and in the end the only
spark I'll see is
silly point.

PURE POST

The window-cleaners piped
water from a purifier
in their van. They only did
the outside but the view
was clear enough for us
to see and see again pure
world outside as though
our windows were wide open,
which most of them aren't
built for so we can't let
in or out our noticing
when something like a gatepost
with no gate on one side
and no fence on the other
seems if not strangely
beautiful beautifully strange.

BACK-LICKING

I'm watching an ordinary
grey cow that needs its back
if not scratching licking.
Maybe all cows have necks
so multi-jointed they can turn
and lick themselves on the back.
I'm not into licking but I need
to swivel quietly round
and catch myself and what's
in the field behind me
unaware. Legs folded under it,
head thrust (if cows were us)
mournfully, beautiful grey cow.

AS GOLDFINCHES

As goldfinches take care
to pause in nearby bushes
before darting out
to peck at sunflower hearts
and spit away the husks

so trains from Paddington
are careful or they used to be
to pause beside a cemetery
until the signal nods
and lets them into Oxford.

Always check on the dead
is good advice. Make sure
your parents are as you left them
in your nearby mind,
lovingly remembered and

forgotten. Hearts and husks.

WORK IN PROGRESS

Looks like grief in progress,
the wheelbarrow abandoned
half-way down the garden,
half-way across. Was it
on its way to being tipped
up, left leaning forward
on a shed with paint-pots,
an old cupboard, broken chairs
inside? Was grief suddenly
too much to push around?
What sometimes works with grief
and wheelbarrows is turning round
and pulling, taking the weight
behind you till you're almost
happy knowing by heart.

LEG BEFORE

I don't know how it got there
but when my desk-top opens
a full-length photograph comes up
of the great W.G.Grace
well past his prime by now
raising his bat in disdain.

There's someone keeping wicket
with a brown belt just like Grace's.
There's deep fine leg. There's
a sheepish man who's had enough
of being where long stop was.
They're always there. It must be 1900.

When I log out I see
the big man's boot is in the way.
My cursor can't shut down.
He's plumb in front, he
always is. Sometimes I feel
like muttering, well how's that?

THE LOG-MAN
for Peter Rowe died 31.8.20

I see now
you wanted to complete
your log-collection

sawed and barrowed in
from the wood
and piled

immaculately
in your garage either side
of the car.

When both sides reached the ceiling
you must have known
you'd done enough.

Computers weren't for you
but for a few more years
you went on

waiting in your chair
logged-on and lovely
for the rest of us.